The Cloud Mountain Minnows Keeper's Handbook

A Step-by-Step Guide to Raising these Beautiful Fishes No Matter Your Experience Level, Their Natural History, Habitat, Behavior, and Ultimate Care

KYLER NICHOLAS

DEDICATION

To My Lovely Wife Olivia Without
Whom I Would Never Have Had
The Courage To Do The Thing I
Loved The Most

Table of Contents

Chapter

1

Introduction to White Cloud Mountain Minnow

Tanichthys albonubes, or the White Cloud Mountain Minnow, is a species of freshwater fish found only in the White Cloud Mountains of China. They are a favorite among fish tank keepers due to their calm demeanor and shiny silver coloring. Because of their resilience, white cloud mountain minnows are a great pick for a community aquarium or a planted tank.

The maximum length for a White Cloud Mountain Minnow is about 2 inches. Their bodies are slender and lengthy, and they are a shiny silver tint that can reflect blue or green under certain lighting conditions. One of the telltale signs of this species is a small, black mark near the base of the dorsal fin.

White Cloud Mountain Minnows are found naturally in mountain streams and rivers; these fish do best in chilly water (60–70 degrees Fahrenheit) with a pH of 6-7. These fish are remarkably tolerant, thriving in a variety of environments, however they do best in water with a strong current and plenty of oxygen.

White Cloud Mountain Minnows require a tank environment that is as close to their natural habitat as possible. Maintain a pH of 6.0–7.0 and a temperature of 60–70 degrees Fahrenheit in their tank at all times. The tank's temperature can be maintained with the help of a heater. Due to their small size, a group of 6-8 fish should have at least 10 gallons of tank space. They also want a planted tank with lots of places to hide and jump out of.

White Cloud Mountain Minnows, like other minnows, are docile and won't bother other fish in the tank. Males and females can be maintained together in the same tank because these fish are not territorial.

White Cloud Mountain Minnows are a hardy, low-maintenance fish that would do well in a group aquarium. With the right attention and care, these fish may be a low-maintenance and fun addition to any aquarist's collection, as well as being quite quiet and energetic.

Chapter

2

The History And Natural Habitat Of White Cloud Mountain Minnows

Located in the White Cloud Mountains of China, the White Cloud Mountain Minnow (Tanichthys albonubes) is a species of tiny, freshwater fish. The cyprinid family, of which these fish are a part, also includes such common aquarium favorites as goldfish and koi.

Dr. Klaus Linke, a German biologist, discovered the White Cloud Mountain Minnow in 1932. These fish have apparently been hidden away in the mountains for millennia, which has allowed them to evolve into a distinct species.

White Cloud Mountain Minnows can be found in rivers and streams with a moderate to fast current and clear water. They thrive in water that is between 60 and 75 degrees Fahrenheit and has a pH of 6.5 and 7.5. In the wild, these fish consume both animal and plant stuff, as they are omnivores.

White Cloud Mountain Minnow populations have declined due to overfishing in the past for the aquarium trade. These fish were once critically endangered, but with to conservation initiatives and successful captive breeding, they are now readily available in the aquarium trade.

White Cloud Mountain Minnows can still be found in their natural habitats outside of captivity, despite their widespread use as aquarium favorites. They are utilized in traditional Chinese medicine and as a popular sport fish in China.

The White Cloud Mountain Minnow is a fascinating and distinctive species with a long and interesting background and diverse natural environment. In the next chapters, we'll go into detail about what it takes to keep these stunning fish healthy and reproduce in your own aquarium.

Chapter

3

Choosing The Right Tank Setup For Your White Cloud Mountain Minnows

A home aquarium for White Cloud Mountain Minnows requires careful consideration of several things to ensure the fish's health and comfort.

Getting the correct sized tank is the first step in keeping White Cloud Mountain Minnows as pets. These fish reach a maximum size of 2 inches, therefore a 10 gallon tank should be adequate for a small community. However, it is safer and easier to maintain a larger tank, so don't be afraid to go with that option if you're on the fence.

A high-quality, effective filter is crucial for maintaining clean, oxygenated water. Due to their susceptibility to water contamination, White Cloud Mountain Minnows require a high-quality filter to ensure their survival.

It's also crucial to make sure your White Cloud Mountain Minnows have plenty of interesting decorations and hiding spots to investigate. Fish will thrive in an aquarium with live plants, PVC pipes, and other aquarium-safe decorations.

White Cloud Mountain Minnows do best on substrates of fine-grained gravel or sand. As bottom-dwellers, these fish will prefer a more forgiving surface on which to swim and feed.

Finally, before introducing your White Cloud Mountain Minnows, you should fully cycle your tank. The goal of this procedure is to build a bacterial colony that can decompose garbage and keep the water clean.

Overall, your White Cloud Mountain Minnows will grow and be a joy to watch and care for with a well-planned tank design and regular maintenance.

Chapter

4

Understanding The Behavior And Personality Of White Cloud Mountain Minnows

Their calm demeanor is one of the main selling points for White Cloud Mountain Minnows among aquarium keepers. These fish are docile and can coexist well with other species of similar temperament. They are lively and inquisitive, which makes watching them a pleasure.

White Cloud Mountain Minnows are a schooling species, meaning they thrive when housed in groups of six or more. They may become anxious and withdrawn if kept separately or in small groups. If you have a tank large enough, you can watch your White Cloud Mountain Minnows swim in an elegant school.

Mount White Clouds In the same way that they will eat almost anything, minnows are also opportunistic feeders. They eat bugs, worms, and plants in the wild, and they'll eat just about anything you put in your aquarium, from flakes to pellets to live or frozen fare.

White Cloud Mountain Minnows are highly attuned to and vulnerable to environmental fluctuations and stress. Maintaining consistent water quality, temperature, and nutrition is crucial to the health of these fish.

White Cloud Mountain Minnows, in general, are an excellent addition to any community aquarium because they are beautiful and little maintenance. You may enjoy these lovely fish for a long time if you know how to care for them properly.

Chapter

5

Proper Feeding And Nutrition For White Cloud Mountain Minnows

White Cloud Mountain Minnows, like all fish, require a diet rich in specific nutrients in order to thrive. Because of their ability to consume both animal and plant stuff, these fish do best when fed a broad diet.

White Cloud Mountain Minnows get their nutrition from a wide range of insects, worms, and plant materials in the wild. These fish can thrive on a diet of high-quality flakes or pellets in a home aquarium. You can augment their diet with live or frozen meals like brine shrimp, daphnia, and mosquito larvae.

White Cloud Mountain Minnows, like all fish, require a

varied diet to ensure they get the proper vitamins and minerals. Fish waste and water quality can be negatively impacted by overfeeding or feeding a diet too high in protein.

White Cloud Mountain Minnows require a once- or twice-daily meal, the quantity of which depends on the tank's volume and the number of inhabitants. You should only give your fish as much food as they can eat in a few of minutes.

In general, you can promote your White Cloud Mountain Minnows' health and lifespan by feeding them a diet rich in a variety of nutritious foods.

Chapter

6

Breeding White Cloud Mountain Minnows

White Cloud Mountain Minnows are an excellent choice for enthusiasts looking to breed their own fish because of how enjoyable the breeding process is and how simple it is to get started.

Creating a dedicated breeding tank is the first step in multiplying your White Cloud Mountain Minnow population. Gentle filtration can be provided by a sponge filter in a tank of at least 20 gallons, and a substrate of fine-grain gravel or sand is preferred. The females will need a safe spot to deposit their eggs, so make sure there are lots of concealing objects available, like PVC pipes or clay pots.

White Cloud Mountain Minnows thrive in water with a pH between 6.5 and 7.5 and a temperature between 72 and 78 degrees Fahrenheit. The health of the fish and their eggs depends on constant water quality and temperature during the breeding phase.

Choose fish that are healthy, well-fed, and have good colour when selecting breeding stock. Mount White Clouds Due to the lack of sexual dimorphism in minnows, it might be difficult to tell males from females only by looking at them. Males are often smaller and more brightly colored than females.

The next phase, after preparing a breeding tank and selecting breeding stock, is to encourage mating. To do this, the tank temperature can be lowered to between 68 and 72 degrees Fahrenheit, and the frequency of feedings can be increased. Breeding behavior can also be prompted by providing live or frozen items like brine shrimp or daphnia.

When the time comes, the females will use the nesting boxes to lay their eggs. by three to five days, the eggs will hatch, and by a week, the fry will be able to swim freely. Fry require a steady supply of fresh or frozen food, and the water quality must be closely monitored.

Breeding White Cloud Mountain Minnows is an enjoyable and gratifying endeavor that can give aquarium lovers years of entertainment. These lovely fish can be bred and raised in a home aquarium with some research and preparation.

Chapter

7

Caring For And Raising White Cloud Mountain Minnow Fry

The focus of your attention should move from the spawning process to the care of the eggs and fry of your White Cloud Mountain Minnows. The health and development of your baby fish depends on the quality of care you provide them with now.

White Cloud Mountain Minnow fry require a specific habitat in which to thrive. A breeder box or a small tank equipped with a sponge filter is ideal for rearing the fry. Fry will feel more at ease if they have access to stable water quality and temperature, and if they have plenty of places to hide.

If you want your fry to grow and develop healthily, you need offer them a variety of foods. Brine shrimp and daphnia, both of which may be purchased live or frozen, are excellent sources of nutrition for the fry. Crushed flake or commercial fry food is another option. Fry have small stomachs and are easily overfed, therefore it's best to feed them several times a day in modest amounts.

Eventually, the fry will outgrow their current tank, and you'll need to feed them a wider variety of foods. It's also crucial to keep an eye on their development and health, and be ready to deal with any potential problems.

If you feed and care for your White Cloud Mountain Minnow fry properly, they will mature into beautiful adults. Enjoyment that lasts a lifetime can be had from raising these stunning fish from fry to maturity.

Chapter

8

Common Health Issues In White Cloud Mountain Minnows And How To Prevent Them

White Cloud Mountain Minnows, like any fish, are susceptible to specific health disorders that can occur from a suboptimal environment or treatment. By learning about these illnesses and implementing preventative measures, you may make a positive impact on your fish's health and longevity.

Stress is a major contributor to White Cloud Mountain Minnow illness. These fish are highly susceptible to stress caused by variations in their water quality, temperature, or nutrition. White Cloud Mountain Minnows show symptoms of stress such listlessness, a diminished appetite, and a visual shift. It's crucial to keep your fish in a stable and consistent environment with consistent water parameters to keep them from being stressed.

White Cloud Mountain Minnows frequently suffer from fin rot as well. The fins become ragged and frayed as a result of a bacterial infection. Poor water quality or fin damage are common causes of fin rot, which can be remedied by increasing the amount of beneficial bacteria in the water and using antibacterial medication.

Mount White Clouds Parasites like ich and anchor worms can also affect minnows. Fish infected with these parasites may itch, flash, and lose their appetite. If you want to keep your fish tank parasite-free, you should quarantine any new additions and check for parasites on a regular basis. If parasites are present, a course of medication can kill them.

Overall, you can do your best to protect your White Cloud

Mountain Minnows from harm by learning about potential health problems and implementing preventative measures.

Chapter

9

Adding White Cloud Mountain Minnows To A Community Tank

Adding White Cloud Mountain Minnows to a community tank? Here are some things to keep in mind for a stress-free introduction.

The first step in keeping White Cloud Mountain Minnows is picking out other fish who will get along with them. These fish are docile and can coexist well with other species of the same temperament. Because of the potential for stress and conflict, White Cloud Mountain Minnows should not be housed with fish of a larger or more aggressive species.

When deciding to introduce White Cloud Mountain Minnows to your community, the size of your tank is an essential factor. These fish only reach a maximum size of 2 inches, so they need plenty of room to swim and thrive. White Cloud Mountain Minnows should be kept in a tank that is at least 10 gallons in size.

White Cloud Mountain Minnows thrive in water with a pH between 6.5 and 7.5 and a temperature between 60 and 75 degrees Fahrenheit. Before adding White Cloud Mountain Minnows, check that your aquarium's water parameters are within this range.

White Cloud Mountain Minnows are omnivores that can be fed a wide variety of meals, including flakes, pellets, live fish, and frozen treats. If you care about the health and happiness of the fish in your community tank, you should feed them a varied diet.

In conclusion, White Cloud Mountain Minnows may be a wonderful addition to any community tank with only a little amount of preparation and care. These little fish are a pleasure to keep because of their bright colors, lively personality, and inquisitive temperament.

Chapter

10

Conclusion: Why White Cloud Mountain Minnows Make A Great Addition To Any Aquarium

Finally, White Cloud Mountain Minnows are a stunning addition to any aquarium because of how simple they are to maintain. Native to China's White Cloud

Mountains, these little fish are renowned for their beautiful colors and calm demeanor.

White Cloud Mountain Minnows are a stunning addition to any aquarium because of their striking appearance and low maintenance requirements. They are social fish that thrive in groups and won't bother your other calm fish if you keep them together. These fish are omnivores as well, eating a wide variety of diets including flakes, pellets, live, and frozen fare.

White Cloud Mountain Minnows are a popular aquarium fish because they are simple to breed and care for at home. Successfully breeding and raising these stunning fish will allow you to experience the rewarding process of watching them flourish.

White Cloud Mountain Minnows, in general, are an excellent addition to any community aquarium because they are beautiful and little maintenance. These lovely tiny fish will add a splash of color and character to your aquarium, whether you're an experienced fishkeeper or just getting started.